Tour of Denver's Buildings AND Monuments

JACK A. MURPHY

HISTORIC DENVER, INC.
DENVER MUSEUM OF NATURAL HISTORY

This project was partially funded by a State Historical Fund grant award from the Colorado Historical Society, and with the assistance of Historic Denver, Inc.

This edition does not contain citations and has an abbreviated bibliography. For researchers wanting further information, an expanded manuscript with citations is on file at the Denver Museum of Natural History library.

Cover photo: Denver City and County Building by Ken E. Erickson © 1995 DMNH
Photos on pages 4–5 by Gary Hall © 1995 DMNH
Photos on pages 14–16 by Rick Wicker © 1995 DMNH

International Standard Book Number: 0-914248-06-5
Copyright © 1995 Denver Museum of Natural History

Published by
Historic Denver, Inc.
821 17th St., Suite 500
Denver, Colorado 80202

in cooperation with
Denver Museum of Natural History
2001 Colorado Blvd.
Denver, Colorado 80205

Printed in Colorado by Select Printing.

Editor: James T. Alton
Design and Composition: Cathy Holtz

CONTENTS

Acknowledgments

I am indebted to Bob Woodhams and Ken Erickson, Department of Earth Sciences volunteers at the Denver Museum of Natural History, for their continued interest and commitment to this project. For a number of years, we have worked together documenting and describing geological aspects of Denver's stone buildings for Museum field trips and programs. In addition to photographic documentation and cataloging, Bob Woodhams continues to be invaluable in many aspects of research and development for this ongoing project. Ken Erickson has photographed every building with the geology of the materials in mind as well as with an artist's eye. Many thanks are also extended to the helpful personnel of both the Denver Public Library's Western History Department and the Colorado Historical Society. I owe special thanks to Bob Akerley, Robert Dameraua, Elvie Davis, Nora Fisher, Julie and Darvin Hendee, Corinne Hunt, Kirk Johnson, Dan Liesveld, Jim MacLachlan, Cath Murphy, Tom Noel, Marian Ramsey, Tito Rael, Glenn Scott, and Ann Student.

INTRODUCTION

Welcome to a tour of thirty-two buildings and monuments in downtown Denver—really a geology field trip in disguise. My approach differs from that of other tours: I focus on the geological aspects of the region, emphasizing the handsome stones from which these structures were built. Many of the sites are also important historic buildings designated by the Denver Landmark Preservation Commission Register or listed in the National Register of Historic Places.

This self-guided tour covers about two miles, so you can walk, bike, or drive. Public transportation can readily be used as part of the route parallels the 16th Street Mall.

A number of geological questions can be asked along the route: What is Denver's geologic setting? What stones are used in the buildings? Where do these rocks originate, and how old are they? How do these rocks relate to Colorado's geologic history? By the end of this book, you should have some answers.

In addition to investigating the geology and identifying the rocks and minerals of these structures, there are other engaging subjects to explore pertaining to regional history, art, and architecture. The books listed as recommended reading discuss these topics. They are also covered in programs and field trips offered each year by the Denver Museum of Natural History, the Colorado Historical Society, Historic Denver, Inc., and Colorado Preservation, Inc.

FIGURE 1. FOR A GEOLOGIST, CORRECTLY IDENTIFYING BUILDING STONES REQUIRES SEEING THEM FIRST IN THE FIELD. LYONS SANDSTONE CAN BE FOUND IN NUMEROUS OUTCROPS LIKE THESE ALONG THE FRONT RANGE.
PHOTO: JACK A. MURPHY
© 1995 DMNH

Taking a Geology Field Trip

If we were taking a geology field trip to the mountains, we would want to find out what kind of rocks occur at a particular place, how old they are, and what they tell us about the geologic history of the area (Figure 1). We would locate and identify typical rocks and would search for telltale fossils, crystals, or sedimentary structures. Knowing what rocks look like in the field allows us to identify them elsewhere. You will see rocks from the foothills and mountains in downtown Denver buildings and monuments (Figure 2).

FIGURE 2. THE U.S. MINT, CITY AND COUNTY BUILDING, DENVER CARNEGIE LIBRARY BUILDING, AND STATE CAPITOL (SEEN HERE IN THE 1930s) ALL CONTAIN STONE FROM COLORADO QUARRIES. PHOTO: COURTESY OF COLORADO HISTORICAL SOCIETY

Rocks used for commercial purposes are often just called *stones*, or *building stones*. Some are so well known that their geological identity or source location is reflected in their name—for example, Lyons Sandstone or Pikes Peak Granite. Others, such as *Yule marble*, have been given a trade name by the building stone industry. These names appear in italics throughout the book.

A few other useful terms: *Dimension stone* is rock cut into regular-sized blocks for use in walls, windows, and stairs. *Flagstones* are two-to four-inch-thick slabs of sandstone used in sidewalks, building walls, and steps.

Although fossils are rare in building stones, some shells of marine mollusks appear on the tour (stop 5). The black fernlike patterns, or dendrites, often seen in Lyons Sandstone are not plant fossils. They are iron or manganese stains deposited by groundwater along a bedding plane of the stratified sandstone.

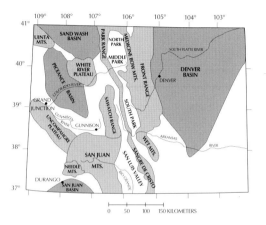

FIGURE 3. COLORADO'S GEOLOGY FORMS A MOSAIC OF UPLIFTED MOUNTAIN RANGES AND LOW-LYING BASINS NOW PARTIALLY FILLED WITH SEDIMENT. BASED ON TWETO (1987), P. 5.

A magnifying glass and a simple rock and mineral book are about all you might need for this trip. To see a wide range of common and exotic rocks beforehand, visit one of the stone yards or monument distributors listed in the telephone book or go see the rock and mineral exhibits at the Denver Museum of Natural History and the Geology Museum at the Colorado School of Mines in Golden. Also, several gem and mineral clubs in the area organize programs, field trips, and gem and mineral shows. For more information, write to the Greater Denver Area Gem and Mineral Council, P.O. Box 621444, Littleton, CO 80162.

REGIONAL GEOLOGY

Denver's Civic Center presents an excellent location from which to discuss this region's geology, including Colorado's mountain ranges and adjacent basins (Figure 3). The earth's crust has been significantly uplifted into mountain ranges twice during Colorado's geologic history—once about 300 million years ago and again beginning 66 million years ago. In between uplifts, the continental interior was a moderately stable area of low relief. During each mountain-building episode, the

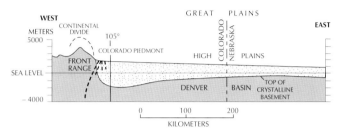

FIGURE 4. Cross-section of the 12,000-foot-thick Denver Basin, from west to east. The vertical scale is exaggerated. Based on Hansen and Crosby (1982), p. 31.

sedimentary rocks (sandstone, shale, and limestone) covering the region were stripped off by erosion, exposing the core Precambrian crystalline rocks (gneiss, schist, and granite). Many valuable mineralized veins and industrial rocks and minerals were thus revealed. The present configuration of Colorado basins and ranges formed during the second period of mountain-building activity, the Laramide Orogeny.

The Denver Basin

Beneath us is the large Denver Basin, a north-south-trending, elongated, centrally depressed feature that formed when the Front Range was uplifted 66 million years ago. The deepest part of the basin lies beneath Denver. Some twelve thousand feet of stratified sandstones, shales, limestones, and clays are preserved here, sitting on top of Precambrian schist and gneiss (Figure 4). These rocks range in age from Paleozoic to Tertiary (Figure 5) and represent sediments that were deposited in many different environments in this part of North America over the last 600 million years. Much of the Denver Basin contains sediments that are rich in petroleum, natural gas, coal, uranium, sand, and gravel, plus enormous quantities of groundwater.

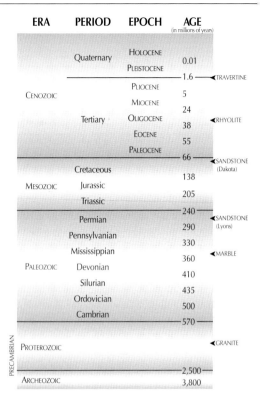

FIGURE 5. The geologic time scale. Important Colorado building stones and their approximate ages are indicated on the right.

ERA	PERIOD	EPOCH	AGE (in millions of years)	
CENOZOIC	Quaternary	HOLOCENE	0.01	
		PLEISTOCENE		
			1.6	◄ TRAVERTINE
	Tertiary	PLIOCENE	5	
		MIOCENE	24	
		OLIGOCENE	38	◄ RHYOLITE
		EOCENE	55	
		PALEOCENE		
			66	◄ SANDSTONE (Dakota)
MESOZOIC	Cretaceous		138	
	Jurassic		205	
	Triassic		240	
PALEOZOIC	Permian		290	◄ SANDSTONE (Lyons)
	Pennsylvanian		330	
	Mississippian		360	◄ MARBLE
	Devonian		410	
	Silurian		435	
	Ordovician		500	
	Cambrian		570	
PRECAMBRIAN — PROTEROZOIC				◄ GRANITE
			2,500	
ARCHEOZOIC			3,800	

Geology in Denver's Backyard

We can easily see most of the 12,000-foot-thickness of rocks contained in the Denver Basin. These rocks are tilted and exposed in hogback ridges and outcrops along the mountain front at Red Rocks Park and Dinosaur Ridge, west of Denver (Figure 6). The once flat-lying rock formations, dating from the Pennsylvanian to Cretaceous Periods, are upturned at angles of 45 degrees or more and dip eastward into the Denver Basin. The rocks were displaced from their horizontal position during the Laramide uplift of the Front Range. The oldest sedimentary rock west of Denver is the Pennsylvanian-age Fountain Formation. It was deposited directly on an ancient erosion surface of Precambrian gneiss and schist. The contact between these two rocks of different

FIGURE 6. GENERALIZED CROSS-SECTION OF THE DENVER BASIN, FROM WEST TO EAST, SHOWING ROCK LAYERS FOUND WEST AND SOUTH OF DENVER. ROCK FORMATIONS QUARRIED FOR BUILDING STONES ARE LISTED. BASED ON SCOTT (1963), P. 4.

ages represents a great *unconformity*; rocks representing the Cambrian through Mississippian Periods are missing because they were either eroded or not deposited. A bronze plaque near the upper parking lot at Red Rocks Park marks one point where this unconformity is visible.

The younger Denver Basin rocks, the Cretaceous-age shales and sandstones that formed when the ocean last covered the North American interior, are seen to the east of the hogbacks. Highway C-470 goes through this region. Sea level receded when the Laramide Orogeny began.

After the Laramide Uplift

Conglomerates, sandstones, and shales were eroded from the mountains and deposited across the region as the Front Range was slowly uplifted. The oldest of these deposits, the Cretaceous-age Arapahoe Formation and the Cretaceous-Paleocene–age Denver Formation, are our local bedrock. The Denver Formation is several hundred feet thick in some places. The upper parts of it can be found exposed in stream valleys from Denver to Golden, especially along Bear Creek, Clear Creek, and the west side of the South Platte River. This formation varies in composition from place to place but is generally orange-brown sandstone, conglomerate, and fine-grained sediment, such as siltstone and claystone. Excavations at Denver International Airport uncovered well-preserved fossil palms and sycamore trees from the Denver Formation, indicating that a warm climate supported subtropical vegetation here during the Late Cretaceous.

Where the Mountains Meet the Plains

Denver, Colorado Springs, and Fort Collins are located where the Great Plains join the Rocky Mountains in an area called the Colorado Piedmont. Toward the end of the Tertiary, the surface of the land was continuous from the plains to the mountains. Sculpting of the Colorado Piedmont created the present landscape during the Pleistocene, the famed Ice Age. The Ice Age originated with climatic changes about three million years ago. The changing climate and the resulting advances and retreats of glaciers in the mountains

FIGURE 7. DOWNTOWN DENVER, AS SEEN FROM THE AIR IN EARLIER DAYS PHOTO: COURTESY OF COLORADO HISTORICAL SOCIETY

controlled cycles of erosion and deposition on the old Tertiary surface. There is no evidence that glaciers extended out of the mountains onto the plains; however, streams carried glacial outwash and deposited it across the region.

Denver's Ice Age Hills and Valleys

An aerial view of Denver reveals a landscape of low relief, difficult to see because of all the buildings and trees (Figure 7). Denver's topography is comprised of broadly rolling hills and stream valleys.

The level of the land increases in elevation westward and eastward away from the South Platte River valley. To the east, this upland surface merges with the Great Plains beyond Denver International Airport. Various unconsolidated sediments deposited during the Late Pleistocene cover this area, sometimes in thicknesses of up to one hundred feet. These surficial deposits include clay, silt, sand, gravel, and fine-grained, windblown (eolian) sand. Many Pleistocene fossils have been discovered in these sediments during excavations at construction sites, including skeletal remains of horses, camels, peccaries, a musk ox, mammoths, and various small rodents.

The Broadway Terrace

The flat expanse of land below Capitol Hill, from Civic Center through downtown Denver, is the old floodplain of the South Platte River—a topographic feature locally known as the Broadway Terrace. The Broadway Terrace formed during the Pleistocene when thick deposits of sand and gravel, the Broadway Alluvium, accumulated in the channel of the South Platte River. All of downtown Denver is built on this alluvium. The caissons for high-rise buildings are sunk fifty to seventy feet down through this material into the bedrock of the Denver Formation.

BUILDING STONES ON THE TOUR

Rocks are composed of one or more minerals, and every rock formed in a specific type of environment at a certain time. Most rocks used in buildings can be easily identified by their physical properties once you begin to recognize them. Properties such as density, hardness, and color are the attributes making rock useful or attractive for commercial and industrial purposes—for building and decoration. Generally, the densest, heaviest, and least porous rocks are the strongest and can often be made to take on an excellent glossy polish.

There are three types of rocks: igneous, sedimentary, and metamorphic. Igneous rocks were molten magma that was either extruded onto the earth's surface by a volcano (forming lava or other material) or intruded into the earth's crust where it solidified and cooled (becoming granite or a similar rock). Sedimentary rocks result when sediments, such as sand or silt, are transported and deposited by water or wind; grains are then cemented together with quartz or calcite to form sandstone, shale, or claystone. Metamorphic rocks are formerly sedimentary or igneous rocks that have been altered or recrystallized by heat and pressure. For example, the sedimentary rock limestone becomes the metamorphic rock marble; likewise, shale becomes slate, and quartz sandstone becomes quartzite.

Five main rocks were quarried locally and used in early Denver buildings: granite, sandstone, marble, travertine, and rhyolite tuff. By the end of this tour, you should have no difficulty in recognizing them all. These rocks come from thirteen key locations around the state.

G R A N I T E . Hard, dense, igneous rocks such as granite form much

of the cores of Colorado's mountain ranges. Along the Front Range, large masses of gray or pink Precambrian granitic rocks can be found west of Boulder, near Silver Plume, and in the Pikes Peak area. Each site represents a different age of intrusion into the earth's crust. Granite is composed of quartz, feldspar, and mica, plus minor accessory minerals such as hornblende. Many building stones are called granite even though they may be another igneous rock.

S A N D S T O N E . Hogbacks and foothills on the margins of mountain

ranges expose thick layers of resistant sandstone. Sandstone formed when quartz and feldspar grains were eroded from Precambrian rocks in the mountains and then transported by streams into channels, alluvial fans, or deltas. Windblown sand was also deposited in sand dunes on ancient deserts or along former seacoasts. In both cases, the grains were then cemented together and buried beneath other sediments, forming flat-lying solidified beds of sandstone and associated rocks. Weathering and erosion exposed these rocks, which became some of Colorado's most important building stones, especially those from Manitou Springs, Morrison, Lyons, Arkins, and west of Fort Collins.

M A R B L E .   Marble is associated with mountain uplift that exposes

metamorphosed limestone or dolomite. Limestone is a chemically precipitated sedimentary rock that originally formed as a limy mud deep in an ocean basin. When subjected to heat and pressure, limestone is metamorphosed into marble. The composition of the material—calcium carbonate—remains the same, but the limestone is recrystallized, forming different grades and colors of marble. Marble of good quality is uncommon.

Many types of metamorphic rocks and minerals are called marble in the building trade. Marble forms mainly from limestone. Slate (from shale) and quartzite (from quartz sandstone) also supply interesting decorative and ornamental stones, but they are technically not marble. Dark green serpentine, known in the building trade as *Verde Antique*, is often called marble, too. You can find marble used in building interiors, as decorative tiles, as stone in fireplaces, and in carvings. Marble is also imported from many foreign localities.

T R A V E R T I N E .   Layers of travertine are built up by hot or cold

springs carrying carbonate and silica in groundwater to the surface. Hence, travertine is usually the last rock formed at a location. Such is the case at Wellsville in Fremont County, where a thick travertine deposit has been quarried for building stones. The minerals composing travertine often originate in a fault zone where underground limestone is dissolved at depth and redeposited as travertine on the surface. When solidified, the stone can be cut into slabs fairly easily and makes attractive, polished floor tiles or wall coverings.

RHYOLITE TUFF. Rhyolite flows and thin layers of ash fall tuff

 originated from volcanic eruptions 35 million years ago in central Colorado. These materials were deposited on a Tertiary erosion surface and now extend as far east as Castle Rock in Douglas County, where they are an important source of building stone. Rhyolite is chemically and mineralogically similar to granite, but rhyolite is an extrusive (flowed from vents or erupted into the air) igneous rock, whereas granite is an intrusive (cooled underground) igneous rock.

Castle Rock rhyolite is one of the most widely used local building stones. Its geological name is Wall Mountain Tuff. It has an attractive tan to gray color. Because of its light color and fine-grained texture, this tuff might be mistaken for limestone. However, you can easily recognize this stone once you observe its characteristics. The very durable, high-silica material breaks with a sharp conchoidal, or curved, fracture. It is commonly used with a rough-hewn surface that causes a constant play of shadows across the walls of buildings.

COLORADO'S BUILDING STONE INDUSTRY

The tectonic forces that uplifted the continental interior into mountain ranges revealed rich mineral veins and exposed important nonmetallic resources: granite and marble for building stones, shale and clay for bricks, limestone for mortar, and gypsum for plaster of paris. Colorado long ranked high in the nation in the production of a variety of rock and mineral commodities as well as oil, gas, coal, and uranium. Sand and gravel for construction are currently the state's leading mineral products.

The best of times for the Colorado dimension stone industry was a short span at the end of the 1800s, when profits from gold and silver mines and railroads were at their peak. A building boom coincided with the existence of Denver's own architectural magazine, *Western Architect and Building News*, published from 1889 through 1891. Shortly thereafter, in 1893, the Sherman Silver Purchase Act eliminated government

FIGURE 8. IN 1867, WORKERS AT A QUARRY NEAR MORRISON PRODUCED BUILDING STONES ENTIRELY BY HAND. PHOTO: DENVER PUBLIC LIBRARY, WESTERN HISTORY DEPARTMENT

subsidies for silver production. Panic seized the economy and construction projects halted abruptly because of this silver crash. The stone industry never regained its former prominence. In the 1900s, concrete replaced stone foundations, walls, and sidewalks, and asphalt supplanted paving stones on streets.

During the better times, people from various backgrounds had established communities near building stone centers throughout Colorado. The art of working with stone, from quarrying to masonry (Figure 8), had to be imported from eastern states. Over the years, the following sites figured prominently in Colorado's building stone industry.

A R K I N S .   The hogbacks on the eastern flank of the mountain front west of Loveland in Larimer County are renowned for excellent brown- and tan-colored Permian-age Lyons Sandstone. This fine-grained, even-bedded sandstone has been used for flagstones and buildings for over a hundred years. It formed in large sand dunes on the margin of ancestral mountains that were uplifted in Pennsylvanian time. Erosion of these mountains continued into the Permian.

PINEWOOD SPRINGS. This quarry, the source of *Colorado Red granite*, is located in Larimer County, a few miles north of Lyons, in 1.4-billion-year-old Saint Vrain Granite. This granite, widely used in monuments, appears on the walking tour at the Colorado Veterans' Memorial (stop 6) and the First Baptist Church (29).

LYONS. Lyons, in Boulder County, is one of Colorado's best known stone centers. Before the 1900s, vast quantities of red-colored Lyons Sandstone were shipped to eastern cities. The sandstone comes from large Permian-age dunes preserved in hogbacks and hills extending into Larimer County. This area remains one of the most important sources of sandstone, which has been used in many Front Range buildings and monuments (such as 6 and 24).

FIGURE 9. WORKMEN FOR THE KERR STONE COMPANY NEAR HOWARD QUARRIED RHYOLITE TUFF. PHOTO: MEIGS, DENVER PUBLIC LIBRARY, WESTERN HISTORY DEPARTMENT

SOUTH PLATTE CANYON. Pikes Peak Granite, dated at 1.0 billion years old, can be found in South Platte Canyon in the Buffalo Creek area of Jefferson County. Although quarries here contained excellent stone that could be cut into large blocks, these operations succeeded because they were on the route of the old Denver, South Park, and Pacific Railroad, which transported the material to Denver. Quarries near Buffalo Creek supplied the coarse-grained, pink-colored granite for the foundation and other parts of many buildings, including the U.S. Mint (2), Denver's Carnegie Library (3), the Kittredge Building (11), the Equitable Building (15), and the Brown Palace Hotel (20).

CASTLE ROCK. Mesa tops in Douglas County are the source for high-quality *Castle Rock rhyolite*. Railroads transported large quantities of this attractive, hard volcanic rock to Denver and beyond. Today, rhyolite is quarried with heavy equipment as an aggregate from the mesa south of town. A small dimension stone company also operates from this quarry, producing rough-hewn blocks the same size as those mined one hundred years ago. Notable historical buildings made of this stone include the Kittredge Building (11) and Trinity United Methodist Church (19).

MANITOU SPRINGS. This historic town, located in El Paso County at the foot of Pikes Peak, was an important source for sandstone. The spectacular tilted strata of Lyons Sandstone and the Fountain Formation at Garden of the Gods extend south of Highway 24 to a long-abandoned quarry on private property in Red Rock Canyon. Early reports refer to this as *Manitou sandstone* from the Kenmuir quarries. This relatively soft, red-orange Permian-age sandstone was used in several Denver buildings, including the Masonic Temple (12), the Boston Building (14), and Central Presbyterian Church (21).

STONE CITY. Fort Carson now occupies this long-forgotten site in Pueblo County, about twenty-five miles northwest of Pueblo. Stone City quarries produced a light-colored, fine-grained quartz sandstone that may be Cretaceous in age. The monuments, walls, and balustrades of Civic Center (4) and the Denver Carnegie Library (3) are made of this stone.

BEULAH. The nearly flat-lying beds west of Beulah, about twenty-five miles west of Pueblo in Pueblo County, contain one small, open pit quarry on private property that produced the wall covering of the State Capitol (27). This quarry mines Upper Mississippian limestone. Its attractive, fine-grained product has often been misidentified as onyx or marble.

COTOPAXI AND TEXAS CREEK. This long-abandoned granite quarry area is located in the heart of the Arkansas River Valley in Fremont County. It supplied 1.4-billion-year-old gray granite for the Colorado Office Building, part of the Denver City and County Building (1), and some of the original U.S. Mint (2).

HOWARD. The obscure Kerr quarry (Figure 9), near Howard in the Arkansas River valley of Fremont County, supplied a stone called white lava for the First Church of Christ, Scientist (28). As far as we know, this rhyolite is an ash flow tuff of Oligocene age that originated from a volcanic source in the eastern San Juan Mountains.

WELLSVILLE. Ten miles east of Salida, in the Arkansas River valley of Fremont County, lies Colorado's largest travertine quarry. Until World War II, it supplied stone primarily for building interiors, such as that of the Denver City and County Building (1).

GUNNISON. Gunnison, located on U.S. 50 in western Colorado, is the site of the Aberdeen quarry, which produced the dark gray granite for the State Capitol (27) and the foundation and steps of the Colorado State Museum (30). This stone, South Beaver Creek Granite, is 1.72 billion years old, making it one of Colorado's oldest rocks.

MARBLE. The nationally acclaimed *Yule marble* comes from the aptly named town of Marble in Gunnison County, some thirty-five miles southwest of Glenwood Springs. Reopened in 1990, the quarry here continues to produce high-grade white marble (Figure 10). Earlier in the 1900s, this stone was used in such significant structures as the Tomb of the Unknown Soldier in Arlington, Virginia, and the Lincoln Memorial in Washington, D.C. Noteworthy *Yule marble* buildings in

Denver include the Cheesman Memorial in Cheesman Park, Colorado National Bank (13), the Old U.S. Post Office (17), U.S. Customs House (18), Colorado Trust–Capitol Life Insurance Building (22), Colorado State Museum (30), and the Colorado State Capitol Annex (31).

FIGURE 10. OVER THE YEARS, COLORADO'S *YULE MARBLE* QUARRIES HAVE PROVIDED HIGH-QUALITY STONE FOR STRUCTURES OF BOTH LOCAL AND NATIONAL IMPORTANCE. PHOTO: U.S. BUREAU OF MINES

THE TOUR

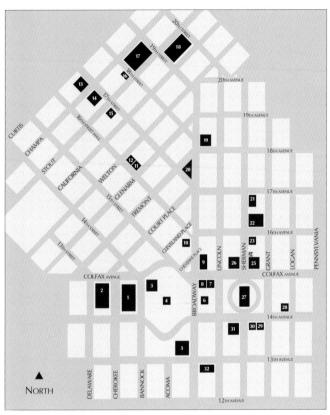

Public rest rooms are located in the RTD Plaza and in restaurants along the 16th Street Mall.

KEY

1   Denver City and County Building
2   U.S. Mint, Denver Branch
3   Denver Carnegie Library Building
4   Civic Center
5   Denver Public Library
6   Colorado Veterans' Memorial
7   Joe P. Martinez Memorial
8   Sadie M. Likens Monument
9   RTD Plaza–16th Street Mall
10   Petroleum Club Building
11   Kittredge Building
12   Masonic Temple
13   Colorado National Bank
14   Boston Building
15   Equitable Building
16   Ghost Building
17   Old U.S. Post Office
18   U.S. Customs House
19   Trinity United Methodist Church
20   Brown Palace Hotel
21   Central Presbyterian Church
22   Colorado Trust–Capitol Life Insurance Building
23   Daly Insurance Building
24   Woodward House
25   Colorado State Office Building
26   Colorado State Services Building
27   Colorado State Capitol
28   First Church of Christ, Scientist
29   First Baptist Church
30   Colorado State Museum
31   Colorado State Capitol Annex
32   Security Life Center

DENVER CITY AND COUNTY BUILDING
14TH AVENUE AND BANNOCK STREET

This grand, four-story granite building, with its concave facade of Doric columns, was completed in 1932 at a cost of $4,649,458. Construction had begun in 1929 using a design created by thirty-nine leading architects, all Denver members of the Allied Architectural Association. Controversial when built, it replaced a popular Victorian stone building at 14th and Larimer Streets. The classical design of the City and County Building was meant to be compatible with that of the State Capitol (27) facing it across Civic Center (4).

This is one of the last large granite buildings erected in Denver. A light gray granite from Cotopaxi in Fremont County was used at the beginning of construction. You can see it in the lower level up to the ledge. To finish the project, builders used a similar-looking granite from Stone Mountain, Georgia. The large columns and the upper parts of the building are made of the Georgia granite, which contains characteristic eyelike mineral aggregates up to two inches in diameter. In these aggregates, a halo of light gray feldspar surrounds a black tourmaline core.

The granite columns are 50 feet tall and 5 feet, 3 inches in diameter. The Corinthian capitals on the portico columns were supposedly carved from 26-ton granite blocks. Overall, it took 14,000 tons of stone to create this structure at a reported cost of $1,518,006. The detail on the stonework is impressive, especially the repetitious square-toothed patterns, or dentils, on the upper cornice. A subtle pink-colored Italian marble, *Fleur de Peche*, decorates the insets on the exterior of the building. The east pediment lacks stone carvings because of cost-cutting measures during construction.

A look inside the City and County Building reveals the outstanding use of Colorado travertine in the walls and nineteen-foot-tall columns in the main lobby on the second floor. The travertine is from Wellsville in Fremont County. According to City and County Building records, these columns are the largest of their kind known. Each one was reportedly created from a block of travertine weighing

UNDER CONSTRUCTION;
(TOP) A STONEMASON
SHAPES ONE OF
THE HUGE BLOCKS
OF GRANITE.
PHOTOS: COURTESY OF
BOB AKERLEY

6,600 pounds. The columns on the upper floors are well-made painted imitations consisting of scagliola, which is finely ground gypsum mixed with glue to mimic natural stone.

The City and County Building interior also contains a variety of decorative marbles. Pink *Tennessee marble* from the Knoxville area covers the floors and stairs and contains black, wavy lines called stylolites. A light pinkish gray Tennessee marble, *Roseal*, appears as trim around the main entrances to offices and in the niches at the ends of the main corridor. Vermont marble is used in baseboards in courtrooms and offices. The black- and gold-veined marble trim in the baseboards in the main corridors comes from Italy. The main vestibule and the drinking fountains contain *Botticino marble*, also from Italy. *Red Lavanti*, which may be Italian, is reported on the floor surface, and *York Fossil* borders the floors of the vestibule. Colorado's white *Yule marble* is used on office counters and in the lavatories. You can find an excellent use of terrazzo (chips of marble and rock in a cement matrix) in the floors.

Be sure to see "Montezuma and the Animals" on the fourth floor. The late Gladys Caldwell Fisher, a well-known Denver artist, carved this large (11 by 6 feet, 2½ tons) stone relief in two panels using lava from near Del Norte in Rio Grande County. The work was installed here in 1934, when this floor housed the galleries of the Denver Art Museum.

A SCULPTED EAGLE
TOPS THE CITY AND
COUNTY BUILDING'S
ORNATE TOWER.

PHOTO:
KEN E. ERICKSON
© 1995 DMNH

2

U.S. MINT, DENVER BRANCH
WEST COLFAX AVENUE AND CHEROKEE STREET

This establishment dates back to Denver's gold mining days. No one knows how many ounces of gold have passed through its well-guarded doors in the years since. The Mint grew out of a private gold coin company, Clark, Gruber, and Company. This firm was purchased by the federal government, which established an assay office here in 1862. The assay office bought gold nuggets and masses of crystallized and wire gold from far and wide. The gold was melted, refined, assayed, and cast into small gold bars. By 1859, the aggregate value of gold and silver deposited annually at this office exceeded $5.6 million. The Mint was officially established in 1895 for the purpose of making gold and silver coins.

The present location was purchased in 1896 for $60,000. Construction of the building started in 1897. Initially, the Cotopaxi district quarries in the Arkansas River valley in Fremont County supplied the granite for the Mint. According to newspaper reports, in September 1898, these quarries employed some 150 men. Fifty other workers shaped the blocks at local granite yards. At some point between 1898 and 1899, the Mint contractor terminated use of the Cotopaxi stone and began using another granite from Arkins, located seven miles west of Loveland. Construction took about five years. Although outfitted with special equipment, the local Mint did not produce coins until 1906.

The five-story, Gothic Renaissance building (only two stories extend aboveground) was expanded using a stone facing of Colorado and Maine granite. Tennessee marble forms the window trimmings, whereas Vermont marble is used in the interior. The base of the perimeter fence on the north and east sides of the Mint is coarse-grained Pikes Peak Granite.

The famous Mint robbery occurred on December 18, 1922. As guards began to unload cash from a Federal Reserve truck into the Mint, bandits leaped out of a passing car, grabbed $200,000 worth of bills, and attempted to make a quick getaway. Shots were fired, killing one guard. Weeks later, the dead body of one of the bandits turned up in a car in a rented garage on Capitol Hill.

BUILDERS ALSO USED
GRANITE FOR A 1936
ADDITION TO THE MINT.

PHOTO: COURTESY OF
COLORADO HISTORICAL SOCIETY

3

DENVER CARNEGIE LIBRARY BUILDING
(City and County Annex 3: Board of Commissioners Building)
WEST COLFAX AVENUE AND BANNOCK STREET

This structure housed Denver's original library, made possible by a $200,000 donation from Andrew Carnegie. It was dedicated February 15, 1910, after three years of construction. It served as Denver's library for forty-six years, and during that time, its elegant, open interior spaces and reading rooms were highly acclaimed. After a new library (5) opened in 1956, this building became home to the Board of Water Commissioners and other city offices.

The Greek Revival–style building sports fourteen impressive Corinthian columns on the north facade. The original staircase at the Colfax Avenue entrance was removed during renovation in the 1950s; a "sunken garden" entrance that drops several feet below ground level replaced it.

The splendid exterior is made of gray-colored *Turkey Creek sandstone*, the same stone used throughout the adjacent Voorhies Memorial and Greek Amphitheater in Civic Center. A foundation of large blocks of Pikes Peak Granite supports the sandstone. This rock is a relatively soft, fine-grained quartz sandstone that, surprisingly, has not deteriorated extensively from weathering over the years.

This sandstone comes from Stone City, located about twenty-five miles northwest of Pueblo. The exact formation quarried is under investigation.

4

CIVIC CENTER
BETWEEN WEST COLFAX AND 14TH AVENUES, BANNOCK STREET AND BROADWAY

Early photographs show that the Civic Center was once crowded with dwellings. As early as 1904, Denver mayor Robert W. Speer planned to create this park and sunken garden area between the City and County Building and Broadway as part of his campaign to beautify Denver.

The walls, columns, and balustrades in the Greek Amphitheater and the Voorhies Memorial are all made from light gray *Turkey Creek sandstone* from near Pueblo—the same stone used in the old Denver Carnegie Library (3). Notice the well-defined sedimentary structures in the sandstone and the patterns of deposition and truncation by subsequent erosion. During renovation of Civic Center structures in the 1980s, some of the balusters (the upright supports in the railings of the Greek Amphitheater) were replaced with Salem Limestone from Indiana. Looking closely, you can see that the sandstone and limestone differ in color and texture. The Salem Limestone also contains small fragments of fossil shells.

The Voorhies Memorial, located on the north side of Civic Center, was designed by William E. and Arthur A. Fisher of Denver. John H. P. Voorhies, a pioneer Colorado mining man, bequeathed the funds for its construction. Ionic columns support this structure's graceful arch. Notice also the faded murals of western animals by Allen True, a well-known Denver artist. Robert Garrison created the sculptures of children and sea lions in the pool within the curve of the arch. The small Emily Griffith Memorial Drinking Fountain nearby is made of a dark, hard igneous rock, the source of which is unknown.

The Colonnade of Civic Benefactors, at the south end of Civic Center, surrounds the stage of the open-air Greek Amphitheater. The colonnade, designed by Marean and Norton of Denver and built in 1919, is in the Ionic order, the same as many classical structures in Greece. It commemorates city benefactors who contributed to Mayor Speer's beautification project. Allen True's fine murals depict early mining and trapping scenes.

THE VOORHIES
MEMORIAL

PHOTO:
KEN E. ERICKSON
© 1995 DMNH

5

DENVER PUBLIC LIBRARY
BETWEEN 13TH AND 14TH AVENUES ON BROADWAY

The new library towers over the original 1956 building, now visible on the north side. This original four-story building, including the two-story, semicircular glass-paneled rotunda, was designed by the Denver firms of Fisher and Fisher and Burnham Hoyt. Light gray Salem Limestone from Indiana covers the structure, and stone trim in the rotunda includes a dark green granite reportedly from Austria.

Today's library, constructed in 1994–95 at an estimated cost of $64 million, features the winner of a national competition: a design by architect Michael Graves and the Denver firm of Klipp, Colussy, Jenks, DuBois Architects. The new building is faced with both natural and manufactured stone. Of the natural stone, two are limestones. The fine-grained tan limestone on the exterior walls and in the interior floors comes from Solnhofen, near Eichstätt, Bavaria, in Germany. This *Jura marble* originated as limy mud in shallow lagoons and contains fossil ammonites up to eight inches in diameter. The green limestone also on walls and in floors contains fossil belemnites and comes from near Frankfurt, Germany. Ammonites and belemnites were soft-bodied mollusks that lived, respectively, in coiled and chambered or bullet-shaped shells.

Another natural stone is *Stony Creek granite* from New Haven County, Massachusetts. Look for this striking, polished wall covering along the base of the building and the columns. It is a Proterozoic-age granite gneiss, a rock of granitic composition including white quartz, large tan-colored orthoclase feldspar crystals, and black biotite. Notice the dark-colored pieces of wall rock contained in the granite gneiss and the lineations of minerals that were formed before the rock solidified.

Manufactured materials enhance the library's appearance. The red and dark green panels covering the upper exterior walls are a durable cast aggregate.

CONSTRUCTION
PROGRESSES IN
SEPTEMBER 1994.

PHOTO: ROGER WHITACRE,
DENVER PUBLIC LIBRARY,
WESTERN HISTORY DEPARTMENT

6

COLORADO VETERANS' MEMORIAL
BETWEEN 14TH AND EAST COLFAX AVENUES, BROADWAY AND LINCOLN STREET

Dedicated in 1990, this Lyons Sandstone obelisk and plaza honors the memory of Colorado's war veterans. The memorial demonstrates a superior use of Lyons Sandstone with both natural and polished surfaces. The stone formed in ancient sand dunes that developed after the erosion of the ancestral Rocky Mountains some 250 million years ago. Iron-bearing minerals contained within impart its red color. The red granite altar stone embedded in the obelisk is *Colorado Red granite* from Pinewood Springs in Larimer County.

PLACE OF HONOR
AND REMEMBRANCE

PHOTO:
KEN E. ERICKSON
© 1995 DMNH

7

JOE P. MARTINEZ MEMORIAL
BETWEEN 14TH AND EAST COLFAX AVENUES, BROADWAY AND LINCOLN STREET

This little-known memorial in front of the State Capitol honors Colorado's first Congressional Medal of Honor recipient from World War II: José P. Martinez of Ault. As a twenty-three-year-old private in the U.S. Army's 32nd Infantry in 1943, "Joe" Martinez led his comrades against the Japanese entrenched on Attu Island, one of the Aleutian Islands off the coast of Alaska. Fighting an uphill battle, Martinez single-handedly destroyed several machine gun nests that were pinning down his battalion. Although he was killed in the clash, his actions paved the way for an American victory.

Denver artist Emanuel Martinez created this statue, which was dedicated in 1988. An exotic decorative stone from Finland called *Baltic Brown* partially covers the monument. This stone is a unique orbicular granite with ovoid shapes formed during crystallization of two types of feldspar.

A Colorado hero

Photo:
Ken E. Erickson
© 1995 DMNH

DEDICATED IN HONOR OF PFC.
JOE P. MARTINEZ
COLORADO'S FIRST CONGRESSIONAL MEDAL
OF HONOR RECIPIENT OF WORLD WAR II

8

SADIE M. LIKENS MONUMENT
SOUTHEAST CORNER OF EAST COLFAX AVENUE AND BROADWAY

This untended 6.5-foot-tall stone monument is dedicated to a woman who devoted years of her life to aiding survivors of the Civil War and other conflicts. The monument has alternating polished and unpolished sides made of a dark-colored, hard granitic material from an unknown source. You can find similar material in other monuments (4), building trim (5), and headstones in regional cemeteries.

After losing her husband, two brothers, and four nephews early in the Civil War, Mrs. Likens became a nurse, caring for the wounded at the Battle of Shiloh and other clashes until the war ended. She moved to Colorado shortly thereafter and became Denver's first police matron at a time when gambling and corruption flourished and women and children had little representation at the city jail. She also helped organize the Women's Relief Corps, an auxiliary of the Grand Army of the Republic. During the Spanish-American War, she again cared for the wounded. The Grand Army of the Republic, Affiliated Orders and Friends erected the monument to her in 1923.

DENVER'S FIRST POLICE MATRON; (RIGHT) THE MEMORIAL TO HER, SET ON THE SIDEWALK ALONG BROADWAY

PHOTOS: COURTESY OF COLORADO HISTORICAL SOCIETY; (RIGHT) KEN E. ERICKSON © 1995 DMNH

9

RTD PLAZA AND THE 16TH STREET MALL
NORTHEAST CORNER OF EAST COLFAX AVENUE AND BROADWAY

The 16th Street Mall begins here at the RTD Plaza and ends a mile away at Market Street. The $76 million mall, constructed in 1982, helped transform this part of downtown from its weary mid-1900s appearance to its modern image. Looking northwest through the canyon of buildings, you may be able to see Longs Peak in Rocky Mountain National Park.

The panoramic view to the south from the upper RTD Plaza encompasses the Civic Center and a few other landmarks. The nearby Pioneer Monument at Broadway and Cheyenne Place marks the path traveled by covered wagons as they completed their journey across the Great Plains on the Smoky Hill North Trail during the Pikes Peak gold rush. Sculptures by Ken Bunn of bighorn sheep and a mountain lion perch on granite bases at the south entrances of the Denver Post Building.

Alternating gray and red granite lies underfoot and is also used decoratively in adjacent walls, benches, and planters. The red stone is *Colorado Red granite* from Larimer County (see also 6 and 29). Two sources provided the gray biotite granite on the plaza and in the mall: The darker gray granite—trade name *Charcoal*—is from Minnesota; the lighter gray granite is reported to be from Massachusetts.

GRANITE BENCHES LINE
THE UPPER RTD PLAZA.

PHOTO:
KEN E. ERICKSON
© 1995 DMNH

10

PETROLEUM CLUB BUILDING
(Colorado State University)
16TH STREET AND BROADWAY

Exotic stone covers the exterior front walls and interior lobby of this building, now the Denver offices of Colorado State University. Built between 1953 and 1957, this fourteen-story skyscraper was one of the first corporate office buildings in upper downtown, and during the unrivaled boom days after World War II, many major oil and gas companies had their headquarters here.

Buildings of this period rejuvenated the international stone industry as evidenced in the use of the lustrous, black rock, known as anorthosite, covering the east wall at the Broadway entrance. The predominant mineral in this Norwegian rock is labradorite feldspar. You can easily recognize this mineral by its beautiful blue and green flashing reflections of light—a property called chatoyancy—best seen here in morning sunlight. This decorative stone is sometimes called labradorite, which is a similar but coarser-grained rock found in Labrador.

Don't miss the lobby of this building, which is covered with black- and gold-veined Italian *Portoro marble*. The dark areas are rich in organic matter. The wavy gold-colored bands may be dolomite, and the white crosscutting veins are calcite.

LUSTROUS
LABRADORITE CRYSTALS
IN THE FACING STONE
HIGHLIGHT THE
GROUND FLOOR OF
THIS SKYSCRAPER.

PHOTO:
KEN E. ERICKSON
© 1995 DMNH

11

KITTREDGE BUILDING
16TH STREET AND GLENARM PLACE

This seven-story granite and rhyolite building, designed by Denver architect Morris Stuckert, stands next to the red sandstone Masonic Temple. These two rough-hewn structures exemplify the use of native dimension stone and the Richardsonian Romanesque style of architecture that was popular in the late 1800s. This eclectic style, employing rounded arches and rock-faced masonry, is credited to the influential Boston architect Henry Hobson Richardson. Several Denver buildings exhibit this architectural expression (see also 19).

The Kittredge Building, built by Denver developer Charles M. Kittredge, features some tremendous stonework. The upper walls are made of *Castle Rock rhyolite*. Note the ornate carvings on cornices and turrets. The lower two floors are Pikes Peak Granite. The large 2.5-foot blocks, elegant ornamental carvings, and polished columns in the front arch are particularly impressive examples of stonework.

THE KITTREDGE
BUILDING IN
HORSE-AND-BUGGY DAYS
(CIRCA 1900)

PHOTO: L. C. MCCLURE,
DENVER PUBLIC LIBRARY,
WESTERN HISTORY DEPARTMENT

12

MASONIC TEMPLE
16TH STREET AND WELTON

This structure represents the few remaining red sandstone buildings downtown (see also 14 and 21). It was designed by Frank E. Edbrooke, one of Denver's leading architects, who helped popularize this rough-surfaced style using native stone (see also 20 and 21). The exterior walls are red-orange *Manitou sandstone* from El Paso County. In the late 1800s, builders favored this Permian-age sandstone because it could be cut into larger blocks than the thin-bedded sandstone from Lyons (which made excellent flagstones for sidewalks). The upper stories visible from the 16th Street Mall have six arched balconies in smooth cut sandstone; the larger arched windows are in rough-hewn sandstone. The foundation blocks are Pikes Peak Granite. The *Colorado Red granite* floors and steps inside the 16th Street entrance to the present building were added when the 16th Street Mall was built.

Be sure to see the magnificent carved sandstone arch at the north entrance, located on Welton. A note in the July 1889 *Western Architect and Building News* stated that this carving was probably Denver's first example of such stonework done after the stone was in place.

Looking at the exterior of the five-story Masonic Temple, one would never guess that a disastrous fire ravaged this historic structure on March 3, 1984. Two-foot-thick walls buckled, and at first it was thought the building would have to be razed. Renovations involved placing a new steel frame inside the original sandstone walls—essentially creating a new building within the old one. A florist who operated a shop on the ground floor was charged with arson for the four-alarm blaze, which caused some $12 million in damage.

THE MASONIC TEMPLE,
AS IT APPEARED
ABOUT 1910

PHOTO: L. C. MCCLURE,
DENVER PUBLIC LIBRARY,
WESTERN HISTORY DEPARTMENT

13

COLORADO NATIONAL BANK
17TH STREET AND CHAMPA

The Colorado National Bank ranks as one of Denver's most impressive *Yule marble* buildings, rivaling the Old U.S. Post Office (17) in both style and grandeur. It was built by the Seerie Brothers, the contractors for many of Denver's stone structures, including the State Capitol (27).

The original building, designed by Denver architects William and Arthur Fisher, is readily identifiable by its Neoclassical style and fluted Ionic columns. This four-story steel beam structure was erected in 1915, with plans for future growth. The 1926 expansion by architects Merrill and Burnham Hoyt used matching *Yule marble* to extend the building along Champa. Several stories were added to the top of the bank in 1963; this addition was contemporary in design. Differences in the architecture and exterior marble facing between upper and lower floors reveal the different generations of the building.

An impressive feature is the large lobby, also of *Yule marble*. Skylights originally illuminated the lobby, but they were covered over by the 1963 addition. Artist Allen True added the large painted murals, "Indian Memories," between 1915 and 1925. In the early 1970s, the twenty-six-story tower was constructed alongside the original building to answer the bank's need for more space. Vermont marble had to be used for the facing because the Colorado marble quarries were then closed.

14

BOSTON BUILDING
17TH STREET AND CHAMPA

Boston architects Andrews, Jacques, and Rantoul designed this 1890 building, originally called the Boston Block. It is the last remaining native sandstone business building on 17th Street.

Early photographs show that the original sandstone was rough cut. The walls were later smoothed—probably because of bits of stone falling off—resulting in the surface seen today. This sandstone is noteworthy for the huge size of the blocks. They contain cross bedding, which is a sedimentary structure created by the deposition of windblown sand. This *Manitou sandstone* from El Paso County is the same stone used in the Masonic Temple (12) and Central Presbyterian Church (21).

THE BOSTON BUILDING
IN THE 1920s

PHOTO: L. C. MCCLURE,
DENVER PUBLIC LIBRARY,
WESTERN HISTORY DEPARTMENT

15

EQUITABLE BUILDING
17TH STREET AND STOUT

This nine-story, Italian Renaissance Revival–style, E-shaped building has long been considered one of Denver's historic treasures. Completed in 1892, it became the western headquarters of the Equitable Assurance Company of New York. Its architects, the Boston architectural firm of Andrews, Jacques, and Rantoul, had sought to create a modern fireproof structure with interiors open to light and fresh air. In its day, the Equitable Building was the showcase of the downtown commercial district and Denver's tallest building. The landmark Daniels and Fisher tower at 16th and Arapahoe surpassed it in 1911.

South Platte Canyon quarries provided the coarse-grained Pikes Peak Granite for this building. Because this is not a steel beam structure, the granite foundation supports the weight of the overlying brick walls and roof. Sandstone from the Fort Collins area was also used in the foundation. Impressive, rough-dressed granite blocks are exposed in the facade of the first two floors. Andrew Garbutt of Boston created the fine carving in granite above the columns of the Roman wreath.

Inside lies a treasure trove of multicolored foreign and domestic marbles (as well as vaulted mosaic ceilings and Tiffany glass). The wall covering on the porches is dark green, white-veined marble from the south of France called *Verde Alps*. At the Stout Street entrance, a wonderful gold-colored, dark-veined, French *Sienna marble* covers the vestibule leading from the porch to the main corridor. The central reception desk and walls of the main corridor up to the second floor are made of this same stone. Floors and stairs are of Vermont marble. Tennessee marbles are used in the corridors of the upper floors, and white, statuary-quality Italian marble can be found in the lavatories.

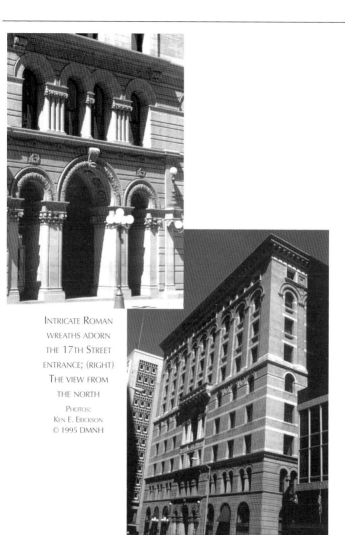

INTRICATE ROMAN
WREATHS ADORN
THE 17TH STREET
ENTRANCE; (RIGHT)
THE VIEW FROM
THE NORTH
PHOTOS:
KEN E. ERICKSON
© 1995 DMNH

16

GHOST BUILDING
18TH STREET AND STOUT

If we wanted to pick a haunted house on the tour, the Ghost Building might be our best bet. This 1895 building was destroyed and then reincarnated, and Mr. Ghost, the original owner, belonged to Denver's Psychical Research Society.

Built with brown sandstone from an unknown source, this picturesque structure originally stood at 15th Street and Glenarm Place. It was built by A. M. Ghost, an early Denver real estate broker. Several businesses occupied the original building, including the office of the man who designed it, acclaimed Denver architect William Lang, and his partner, Marshall Pugh. Over the years, the once proud building became dilapidated and, in the opinion of some, hardly worth renovating.

In January 1979, Public Service Company announced plans to tear down the landmark and expand their adjacent headquarters. By this time, the Ghost Building was Denver's only remaining commercial Victorian-age structure by Lang, and it epitomized the Richardsonian Romanesque style of architecture in vogue at the time of its construction. In addition, other historic landmarks had already been destroyed. In September 1979, local architect Brian Congleton proposed that the six-inch-thick stone facade be dismantled piece by piece and stored until it could be reassembled. Soon afterward, with the cooperation of Public Service Company, the eighty-eight-year-old building was carefully taken apart. In May 1985, Brown-Schrepferman and Company, a longtime Denver real estate investment firm, decided to incorporate the Ghost Building facade into the newly remodeled ten-story Park Place office complex at 18th and Stout.

THE GHOST BUILDING IN
ITS FIRST
INCARNATION AT
15TH AND GLENARM
PHOTO: *THE DENVER POST*

17

OLD U.S. POST OFFICE
(Byron White U.S. Courthouse)
18TH STREET AND STOUT

Made of Colorado *Yule marble*, the grand Old U.S. Post Office has long been recognized as one of Denver's finest Neoclassical stone buildings. It was constructed between 1913 and 1916—about the time production peaked at the quarries at Marble.

The massive Ionic columns on the Stout Street side are especially impressive. The upper walls at each side of this colonnade bear the names of former postmasters general. The names of former attorneys general are inscribed in a similar location on the Champa Street side between 18th and 19th.

Magnificent sculptures of reclining bighorn sheep grace the southwest entrance of this building. Denver artist Gladys Caldwell Fisher created them using Salem Limestone from Indiana. Upon close examination, you can see the difference in color and composition between the limestone and nearby marble.

Architect Michael Barber directed the renovation of this building between 1992 and 1994. At a cost of approximately $27 million, the old main post office was converted into the new Byron White U.S. Courthouse, home of the 10th U.S. Circuit Court of Appeals and its four courtrooms. All of the building's marble was suffering from general wear and tear and chemical deterioration from downtown air pollution. Air filled with sulfur dioxide and water vapor dissolves marble surfaces. Repairing or replacing damaged stone is an expensive and specialized task. Fortunately, the *Yule marble* quarries had reopened in 1990, making it possible to use stone identical to the original in the renovation.

Recent renovations have restored this landmark to its original grandeur.

18

U.S. CUSTOMS HOUSE
19TH STREET AND STOUT

Like the Old U.S. Post Office, the U.S. Customs House is made of Colorado *Yule marble*. However, the Customs House rests on a foundation of granite from Stone Mountain, Georgia, the same stone used in the columns and upper floors of the City and County Building (1). The cornerstone was laid October 30, 1930, and the building was occupied the following summer. The Customs House exhibits the Italian Renaissance Revival style of architecture and was once the largest of Denver's federal buildings.

Architects George Meredeth Musick, Sr. and Temple H. Buell designed the 1937 expansion of this five-story landmark to occupy the full block between 19th and 20th, and Stout and California. Because of their use of *Yule marble*, this addition temporarily revitalized the struggling quarry and mill at Marble.

GEORGIA GRANITE
SUPPORTS COLORADO
YULE MARBLE.

PHOTO:
KEN E. ERICKSON
© 1995 DMNH

19

TRINITY UNITED METHODIST CHURCH
18TH STREET AND BROADWAY

This picturesque church with its spectacular stone steeple represents probably the finest use of *Castle Rock rhyolite* in any Denver building. The church was constructed in 1887, using a design by Robert R. Roeschlaub. Author and historian Richard Brettell considers this structure to be one of Roeschlaub's greatest achievements. The church is historically important as one of the first stone structures in Denver in the Richardsonian Romanesque style of architecture (see also 11 and 16). In fact, its design bears similarities to the archetypal Trinity Church in Boston, created a decade earlier by the influential Boston architect Henry Hobson Richardson.

CASTLE ROCK RHYOLITE
AT ITS FINEST

PHOTO: L. C. MCCLURE,
DENVER PUBLIC LIBRARY,
WESTERN HISTORY DEPARTMENT

20

BROWN PALACE HOTEL
17TH STREET AND BROADWAY

This grand sandstone structure is one of Colorado's most famous historic buildings. Constructed between 1890 and 1892, its unique triangular design brought architect Frank E. Edbrooke considerable acclaim. An illustration of the hotel appeared on the front cover of the May 21, 1892, issue of *Scientific American*, accompanied by an article praising the hotel's many modern aspects.

The Brown Palace was the inspiration of Henry C. Brown, the well-known Denver pioneer who also donated the land for the State Capitol (27). The hotel was among the first buildings in the nation to use steel frame construction. This technology permitted the architect to incorporate into the building a nine-story central rotunda that is as impressive today as it was a century ago.

According to hotel records, the metal framework of cast iron columns and steel beams is covered by a facade of "Arizona sandstone." Although we know a great deal about the hotel's history, the source of this sandstone has been the object of much speculation. Research at the Denver Museum of Natural History indicates that a quarry in Flagstaff, Arizona, in Triassic-age Moenkopi Sandstone may be the source. Potential sources in Colorado have also been investigated.

The stone in the foundation and first floor is Pikes Peak Granite from the South Platte Canyon region. Wonderful relief carvings of animals decorate the building.

The unique green- and gold-banded onyx paneling in the lobby is unrivaled. No other Denver building contains Mexican onyx in large panels such as these. The onyx came from a mine in Torreon, Mexico. By the time the Brown Palace reached completion, 12,400 square feet of the stone—more than had ever been used in a single building—had been incorporated into the lobby, grand salon, and eighth-floor ballroom.

THE UNUSUAL
TRIANGULAR HOTEL,
AS IT APPEARED
BEFORE 1900

PHOTO: DENVER PUBLIC
LIBRARY, WESTERN HISTORY
DEPARTMENT

21

CENTRAL PRESBYTERIAN CHURCH
1660 SHERMAN

Notice that we have traveled uphill to this site. We have also crossed into a different geological setting. Below us lies the flat Broadway Terrace. We now stand at the edge of the Pleistocene upland surface that extends to the Great Plains beyond Denver International Airport.

This lovely red sandstone church, constructed in 1890–92, was designed by Frank E. Edbrooke. After arriving from Chicago in 1879, Edbrooke became one of Denver's most prominent architects. He designed this church just before starting work on the Brown Palace Hotel (20).

Central Presbyterian Church celebrated its one hundredth birthday in 1960. (The congregation met in two other locations prior to construction of this structure.) The magnificent church interior contains two large stone fireplaces that reflect its frontier heritage. The church has its own museum in the basement, the Robert Shepler Heritage Center, with historic photographs certainly worth seeing.

The red sandstone for this and other buildings of the late 1800s (see also 12, 14, and 24) came from the Kenmuir quarries near Manitou Springs in El Paso County. You may notice a difference between the sandstone slabs in the foundation and front stairs and the sandstone blocks in the walls of the church. The stone for the stairs and foundation probably came from quarries in Lyons, not Manitou Springs.

Close inspection reveals that this sandstone is slowly deteriorating because of weathering and erosion by water and wind, just as if these rocks were outcropping in the foothills. Look for sand grains on the sidewalk at the base of the walls. In some places, the sandstone is exfoliating in small pieces.

22

COLORADO TRUST–CAPITOL LIFE INSURANCE BUILDING
1600 SHERMAN

Architect Harry J. Manning designed this classic Greek-style building in 1924 for the president of the Capitol Life Insurance Company, Clarence F. Daly. Exceptional white terra-cotta trim lines the doors, windows, and decorative cornice, and imposing bronze doors guard the west entrance. Elegant *Yule marble* faces this building and is incorporated into the splendid interior. The use of this stone reflects a time when the town of Marble experienced a revitalization in marble quarrying.

This building stands on the former estate of Charles B. Kountze. A forty-room stone mansion, the first of its kind to be built on Capitol Hill, once dominated the site. In 1887, Mr. Kountze's next-door neighbor lived at the north end of the block on Grant Street—in the red sandstone George Schleier Mansion with its distinctive Queen Anne–style, onion-shaped tower. You can only imagine the impressive view of downtown Denver and the mountains they must have had in those days.

Since 1985, the old Capitol Life Insurance Building has been the headquarters of the Colorado Trust, a foundation endowed with the proceeds from the sale of Presbyterian–St. Luke's Medical Center. Its mission is "to promote and enhance the health and well-being of the people of Colorado" by supporting innovative health-oriented studies and projects.

CLASSIC *YULE MARBLE*
OFFICE BUILDING
WHERE A MANSION
ONCE STOOD

PHOTO:
KEN E. ERICKSON
© 1995 DMNH

23 DALY INSURANCE BUILDING
1576 SHERMAN

This contemporary structure, built in 1959, was originally owned by the Capitol Life Insurance Company, headed by Clarence F. Daly, across the street (22). The building features appealing interior and exterior stonework designed by the architect, James Sudler. The west exterior wall, the flower boxes, and the benches are made of tan-colored travertine that probably came from a deposit near Gardiner, Montana, near the north entrance to Yellowstone National Park. Excellent uses of black, iridescent anorthosite can be found behind the fountain and in the lobby of this building. Labradorite feldspar crystals give this stone its beautiful luster.

ONE OF TWO STOPS

FEATURING TRAVERTINE

PHOTO:
KEN E. ERICKSON
© 1995 DMNH

24

WOODWARD HOUSE
1530 SHERMAN

This historic home is representative of many brick and native sandstone houses built on Capitol Hill in the 1880s. The property was first patented in 1867 to Henry C. Brown. According to the National Register of Historic Places, the property changed hands several times until Henry M. Porter sold it to Helen M. (Bassett) Woodward. She was the wife of Benjamin F. Woodward, a well-known businessman who came here in about 1863 and was involved with the construction of the first telegraph line to reach Denver. Mr. and Mrs. Woodward built this house, which was completed in 1889, and lived here until her death in the early 1900s. The State of Colorado eventually purchased the house and transformed it into the headquarters of the state's archives.

Red sandstone columns and blocks are incorporated into the brick construction. The stone bears great similarity to other red-orange sandstones used in Capitol Hill mansions, but none of their sources were documented. The sidewalks in front of this house are typical flagstones of Lyons Sandstone with ripple marks created by wind blowing over sand.

REPRESENTATIVE OF
CAPITOL HILL HOMES
OF THE 1880s

PHOTO:
KEN E. ERICKSON
© 1995 DMNH

25

COLORADO STATE OFFICE BUILDING
201 EAST COLFAX AVENUE

Two corner lots here at Colfax and Sherman were acquired for government office buildings in 1917 for $103,504. On one of these lots, contractors Seerie and Varnum began construction in 1919 of this five-story granite-covered building. Denver architect William N. Bowman had designed the building in Neoclassical style to be in harmony with the State Capitol across the street. The cornerstone was laid June 5, 1920, and the building opened the following year.

The rough exterior granite blocks are reported to be from Cotopaxi in Fremont County. Two bronze mountain lion sculptures by Robert Garrison flank the Colfax Avenue entrance.

The marble interior of this building is elegant, especially the black-and-white checkerboard floor in the first-floor lobby. The architect chose *Botticino marble* for both this feature and the rest of the first floor and Vermont marble for the remainder of the building. Colorado's *Yule marble* quarries were closed at the time. The pink marble wall tiles and trim have characteristic wavy lines, or stylolites, formed when thin layers of silt or clay were incorporated into the sediment as it was deposited. Also notable is the contrasting use of bronze in the doors, stair railings, and chandeliers, highlighted by the large, magnificent glass skylight.

A $4 million remodeling project in 1983–84 made this building a showcase of historic preservation. It now houses the offices of the Colorado Department of Education.

COLORADO STATE OFFICE BUILDING

26

COLORADO STATE SERVICES BUILDING
1525 SHERMAN

This seven-story office building, located on the northwest corner of Colfax and Sherman, was completed in 1959. The need for additional space for state government offices had become critical soon after World War II, and plans for this building date back to 1947. In 1955, the legislature finally authorized $3,425,000 for construction, and George Meredeth Musick, Sr. and Temple H. Buell were selected as the architects. Another two years elapsed before construction began. When Governor Stephen L. R. McNichols dedicated the building on June 14, 1960, the new 180,000-square-foot facility was already considered too small. Many state agencies still had to rent office space elsewhere.

Original specifications called for white *Yule marble* in order to establish a standard building stone. However, because the *Yule* quarries were closed, Vermont marble had to be used. The stone facing on the base of this building is probably coarse-grained *Diamond Pink granite* from Texas. The use of white marble and coarse-textured granite makes this building appear similar in style to the nearby Colorado State Capitol Annex (31).

VERMONT MARBLE AND
TEXAS GRANITE

PHOTO:
KEN E. ERICKSON
© 1995 DMNH

27

COLORADO STATE CAPITOL
EAST COLFAX AVENUE AND SHERMAN STREET

Plans were already under way to make Denver the capital city when Henry C. Brown, later of Brown Palace Hotel fame, donated the land for the statehouse in 1876. Construction commenced in 1888, and an attractive gray granite from South Beaver Creek in Gunnison County was selected. The stone came from the Aberdeen quarry, located about seven miles south of Gunnison. Fred Zugelder of Gunnison discovered the granite and named the quarry Aberdeen after a similar location in Scotland. Removing and transporting the 280,000 cubic feet of stone—including blocks weighing ten to twelve tons each—from this remote site to Denver proved to be an enormous task. Zugelder and a crew of sixty men quarried the granite blocks between 1889 and 1892. The Denver and Rio Grande Railroad extended its narrow-gauge tracks to the quarry at no extra charge, but the stone had to be reloaded onto cars on standard-gauge track at Salida for shipment to Denver. The Colorado legislature appropriated more than $471,000 so that the Gunnison County material could be used. The cornerstone was laid July 4, 1890, with H. A. W. Tabor presiding. Builders used 20,000 different sizes and shapes of blocks to create this structure.

An unusual, colorful, polished wall covering named *Beulah Red marble* remains a highlight of the Capitol's interior. The legislature approved an additional $164,000 for this gray- and pink-banded stone from west of Beulah in Pueblo County. Its source is a small limestone deposit of Mississippian age. The rock contains unique overlapping bands and swirls of iron-stained sedimentary structures throughout a fine-grained matrix. This material has been called both onyx and marble, yet these terms do not correctly describe this complex limestone. Only a few quarrymen worked this small deposit from 1896 to 1906, mainly for the State Capitol. The project totally consumed the material, making it a one-of-a-kind decorative stone.

THE CAPITOL FEATURES
COLORADO BUILDING
STONES; (LEFT)
STONEMASONS SHAPE
GRANITE BLOCKS
FOR THE CAPITOL
ABOUT 1890.

PHOTOS: COURTESY OF
COLORADO HISTORICAL
SOCIETY

28

FIRST CHURCH OF CHRIST, SCIENTIST
14TH AVENUE AND LOGAN STREET

At first glance, the gray stone making up the walls and columns of this impressive domed church may not appear to be particularly significant. However, this unique ash flow tuff represents an ancient volcanic eruption in the Oligocene. You can see small crystals and grains of biotite and quartz as well as dark-colored volcanic rock fragments on the smooth cut surfaces of this stone.

The quarry for this stone, Kerr Gulch, lies in the Arkansas River valley near Howard in Fremont County. John G. Kerr, who was a member of this church in 1917, once owned the quarry. The Kerr Gulch quarry is fairly well documented considering that it produced one of the state's more obscure building stones. The material referred to as "white lava stone" in issues of *Western Architect and Building News* is probably this ash flow tuff.

The Neoclassical-style church with its six large, white, smooth columns was constructed between 1901 and 1906. Architect Frederick J. Sterner of the firm Varian and Sterner designed the church, which was one of the most imposing stone buildings of the day on the crest of Capitol Hill. In 1904, newspapers compared the size and "stateliness" of the main auditorium, built to seat sixteen hundred, to the Mormon Tabernacle in Salt Lake City.

The cornerstone, laid April 10, 1902, is a beautiful light gray granite containing two types of mica, muscovite and biotite, from Concord, New Hampshire—the home of Mary Baker Eddy, the founder of the Christian Science church.

THE CHURCH TODAY;
(BOTTOM) LAYING THE
CORNERSTONE IN 1902

PHOTOS:
KEN E. ERICKSON
© 1995 DMNH;
(BOTTOM) ARCHIVES OF FIRST
CHURCH OF CHRIST, SCIENTIST

29

FIRST BAPTIST CHURCH
14TH AVENUE AND GRANT STREET

The magnificent, polished red granite columns at the north portico of this American Colonial–style church are unrivaled in Colorado. Made of *Colorado Red granite* from Pinewood Springs in Larimer County, they stand 25 feet, 2½ inches tall and are 2 feet, 11 inches in diameter. The architect, George Meredeth Musick, Sr., documented the locality of the stone as "Lyons granite" in a publication for the building's dedication in 1938. He noted that these "were the largest polished granite columns in Colorado" and that "the blocks were quarried and brought to Denver in the rough where they were turned down on a specially erected lathe which was power driven, however, the finishing and polishing was done by hand."

Musick also documented other stone used in the church. The exterior trim around the main entrance is polished pink Tennessee marble, and the stone trim on the exterior of the building and the tower is Indiana Salem Limestone.

SPECTACULAR GRANITE
COLUMNS MARK
THE CHURCH'S
NORTH ENTRANCE.

PHOTO:
KEN E. ERICKSON
© 1995 DMNH

30

COLORADO STATE MUSEUM

(Legislative Services Building)

14TH AVENUE AND SHERMAN STREET

The granite for the foundation of this Neoclassical building came from the Aberdeen quarry in Gunnison County, the same stone used in the State Capitol (27) across the street. The walls are of *Yule marble*. Architect Frank E. Edbrooke designed the building, which was completed in 1916. It was his last commission before retiring at age seventy-five.

Many Denver residents remember the Colorado history and mining dioramas housed on the first floor and the dazzling state mineral collection on the second floor. The museum and its collections relocated to the Colorado History Museum at 13th and Broadway in 1977, and this structure became the Legislative Services Building. The state mineral collection was transferred to the Geology Museum at the Colorado School of Mines in Golden in the mid-1960s.

Note the Lyons Sandstone curbs in this block.

The building early in
its days as a museum

31 COLORADO STATE CAPITOL ANNEX
1375 SHERMAN

This contemporary-style building, with its unique rounded marble corners, was completed in 1940. In 1938, the town of Marble experienced a slight economic revival when up to 125 workers were needed to supply stone from the *Yule marble* quarry for this building. Thereafter, quarrying declined, and Marble became more of a vacation and resort area. As far as we know, this was the last Denver building made of *Yule marble* prior to the quarry reopening in 1990.

IN THE LATE 1930s,
THIS BUILDING
REPRESENTED A
TEMPORARY REPRIEVE
FOR THE *YULE
MARBLE* INDUSTRY.

SECURITY LIFE CENTER
13TH AVENUE AND BROADWAY

The final stop brings us to the oldest rock on the tour. Completed in 1986, this seventeen-story skyscraper features around its base a facing of granite that is more than 2.5 billion years old. Architect Michael Barber, who later oversaw the renovation of the Old U.S. Post Office (17), designed the building for the Security Life of Denver Insurance Company.

The Archeozoic-age *Carnelian granite* comes from Milbank, South Dakota. This area, extending from northeastern South Dakota into Canada, contains our continent's oldest existing rocks—ones that solidified from molten magma 2.5 to 3.8 billion years ago during the early stages of North America's formation. Colorado's oldest rocks are only Proterozoic in age, making them all less than 2.5 billion years old.

Across 13th Avenue from the Security Life Center stands the Colorado History Museum. In addition to featuring both permanent and temporary exhibits, this building houses the Colorado Historical Society and its valuable reference library and archives. Originally, this institution was located a few blocks east in the *Yule marble* Colorado State Museum (30).

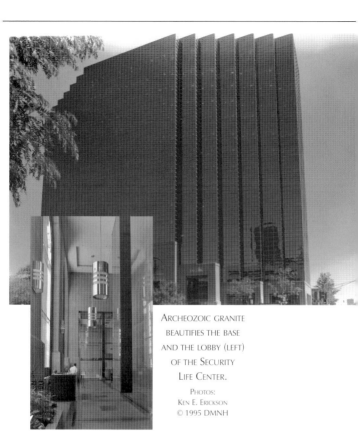

ARCHEOZOIC GRANITE
BEAUTIFIES THE BASE
AND THE LOBBY (LEFT)
OF THE SECURITY
LIFE CENTER.

PHOTOS:
KEN E. ERICKSON
© 1995 DMNH

Organizations Involved in Historic Preservation

HISTORIC DENVER, INC. has gained a national reputation for its work protecting the historical, architectural, and cultural heritage of Denver for the benefit of future generations. For more information, write to Historic Denver, Inc., 821 17th Street, Suite 500, Denver, CO 80202, or call (303) 296-9887.

COLORADO PRESERVATION, INC. is a younger organization, formed in the 1980s. It is dedicated to promoting and advancing the preservation of statewide resources, especially in the mining and agricultural regions of the state threatened by today's changing economies. For more information, write to Colorado Preservation, Inc., P.O. Box 843, Denver, CO 80201, or call (303) 892-9210.

DENVER LANDMARK PRESERVATION COMMISSION is the City and County of Denver agency responsible for identifying, inventorying, and registering important historic Denver buildings. For more information, write to Denver Landmark Preservation Commission, City and County of Denver, Planning and Community Development Office, 200 W. 14th Avenue, Denver, CO 80204, or call (303) 640-4764.

COLORADO HISTORICAL SOCIETY is the organization behind the Colorado History Museum in Denver and regional museums throughout Colorado. It produces publications and sponsors various educational activities for both its members and the general public. For more information, write to Colorado Historical Society, 1300 Broadway, Denver, CO 80203, or call (303) 866-3682.

NATIONAL REGISTER OF HISTORIC PLACES is the U.S. Department of the Interior agency that identifies, documents, inventories, and registers buildings of national significance. For more information, write to Historical Preservation Office, 1300 Broadway, Denver, CO 80203, or call (303) 866-3395.

RECOMMENDED READING

Argall, George O., Jr. Industrial Minerals of Colorado. Quarterly of the Colorado School of Mines, vol. 44, no. 2. Golden, Colo.: 1949.

Ballast, David Kent. Denver's Civic Center: A Walking Tour. Denver: City Publishing Company, 1977.

Brettell, Richard R. Historic Denver: The Architects and the Architecture 1858–1893. Denver: Historic Denver, Inc., 1973.

Chronic, Halka. Roadside Geology of Colorado. Missoula, Mont.: Mountain Press Publishing Company, 1980.

Chronic, John, and Halka Chronic. Prairie, Peak, and Plateau: A Guide to the Geology of Colorado. Denver: Colorado Geological Survey, 1972.

Costa, John E., and Sally W. Bilodeau. "Geology of Denver, Colorado, U.S.A." Bulletin of the Association of Engineering Geologists, XIX (1982), 261–314.

Eitemiller, David J. Historic Tours: The Denver Mint: The Story of the Mint from Gold Rush to Today. Frederick, Colo.: Jande-Hagan Corporation, 1983.

Etter, Don D. "A Legacy of Green: Denver's Park and Parkway System." Colorado Heritage, 1986, no. 3, 9–32.

Fillmore, Barbara J., and Jane D. Dianich. Rock Around the Clock: A Geologic Walking Tour of Downtown Denver. Denver: U.S. Geological Survey, 1992. Available from the GEO Center, Building 20, Room C-2002, MS 914, Box 25046, Denver Federal Center, Denver, CO 80225.

Hansen, Wallace R., and Eleanor J. Crosby. Environmental Geology of the Front Range Urban Corridor and Vicinity, Colorado. U.S. Geological Survey Professional Paper No. 1230. Washington, D.C.: 1982.

Harvey, James R., and Irma Harvey. "The Quarries of the Castle Rock Area." *Colorado Magazine*, vol. 23, no. 3 (May 1946), 114–128.

Hunt, Corrine. *The Brown Palace Story.* Rocky Mountain Writers Guild Publication, 1986.

Jenkins, John T., Jr., and Jannice L. Jenkins. *Colorado's Dinosaurs.* Denver: Colorado Geological Survey, 1993.

Kohl, Edith Eudora. *Denver's Historic Mansions: Citadels to the Empire Builders.* Denver: Sage Books, 1957.

Lowenberg, Robert L. *Castle Rock: A Grass Roots History.* Englewood, Colo.: Quality Press Inc., 1986.

McCollum, Oscar D., Jr. *Marble, A Town Built on Dreams.* 2 vols. Denver: Sundance Publications, 1992–93.

Morris, Langdon E., Jr. *Denver Landmarks.* Denver: Charles W. Cleworth, Publisher, 1979.

Noel, Thomas J. *Denver: Rocky Mountain Gold.* Tulsa, Okla.: Continental Heritage Press, Inc., 1980.

Noel, Thomas J. *Growing Through History with Colorado: The Colorado National Banks, the First 125 Years, 1862–1987.* Denver: Colorado National Banks and the Colorado Studies Center, University of Colorado at Denver, 1987.

Noel, Thomas J., and Barbara S. Norgren. *Denver: The City Beautiful and Its Architects, 1893–1941.* Denver: Historic Denver, Inc., 1987.

Scott, Glenn, R. Quaternary Geology and Geomorphic History of the Kassler Quadrangle, Colorado. U.S. Geological Survey Professional Paper No. 421-A. Washington, D.C.: 1963.

Tweto, Ogden. Rock Units of the Precambrian Basement in Colorado. U.S. Geological Survey Professional Paper No. 1321-A. Washington, D.C.: 1987.

Vandenbusche, Duane, and Rex Myers. *Marble, Colorado: City of Stone.* Denver: Golden Bell Press, 1970.

Walsh, Elaine C., and Jean W. Smith. *Victoria of Civic Center.* Denver: Volunteers of the Colorado Historical Society, 1984.

INDEX

Note: Building citations are listed in **boldface.** Photo citations are noted with "p" following the page number.